WE BELIEVED

Lessons Learned from Jackson's Improbable Run to a State Basketball Championship

Todd Porter

Zac Jackson

Acknowledgements

The authors of "We Believed" owe a debt of gratitude to many people without whom this project would not be possible. We would like to thank Repository Publisher Kevin Kampman, Editor Jeff Gauger and Managing Editor Don Detore not just for their cooperation in reprinting blog entries from cantonrep.com, but also their friendship. The administration of the Jackson Local School District, specifically, Superintendent Cheryl Haschak, Assistant Superintendent Chris DiLoreto, and Athletic Director Terry Peterson for their trust and cooperation. Polar Bears Head Coach Mike Fuline and his coaching staff, who spent countless hours with the authors to make sure details are represented with accuracy and for being a fine role models for their players. The officers and board members of the Jackson Youth Basketball Association for their support and help during this process. Jackson basketball team photographer Jerry Whitehair for his use of the cover picture. Last, and certainly not least, all the players and their families who opened up their homes, their hearts as well as a treasure chest of memories, for the reproduction of this book. Thank you Polar Bears.

Dedications

For the three most important women in my life: Michelle, Sydni and Mom; and my main man, Dylan. I love you all — T.P.

———

To my two favorite semi-slow Manchester point guards of all time, and to their parents and extended families. We're all family and for that, I'm forever grateful — Z.J.

Table of Contents

Introduction

No one wanted it to end. But life goes on and so after the Jackson High School boys basketball team won the Division I state championship, the first team state title in school history, there needed to be a way to remember not just what happened, but why and how it happened. We Believed is a journey down a long four-year process to winning a state title. It is every boy's dream who plays a sport to reach the pinnacle of his high school career. The vast majority of those players fail.

Jackson's Polar Bears, however, did not. They Believed.

We Believed takes you on their journey and how what no one outside Jackson's locker room would have predicted became evident early on in the 2009-2010 Ohio High School Athletic Association's basketball season.

Through hard work and dedication to a common cause, the 2010 Jackson High School boys basketball team won the Division I state title. This is how it happened.

A DEAL IS A DEAL

Josh Egner's run toward a state basketball championship started long before he became the Mohawk-wearing, thunder-dunking, attention-grabbing lightning rod of the 2010 Jackson High School Polar Bears.

This particular run started almost six years earlier, the summer before Josh began the sixth grade.

Josh wanted to play in a local recreational basketball league with his friends at First Friends Church in Jackson. His parents didn't approve. Josh was a gifted player used to playing with and against a higher level of competition. Playing in a community rec league wasn't going to do much for his development.

But he insisted, and promised his parents that he would play hard, take it seriously and get something out of it. Against their better judgment, Gary and Teresa Egner gave their permission.

"We were careful never to push him into anything," said Gary Egner, who coached college basketball before Josh was born. "But when he found something he loved, we encouraged him to take it seriously. I coached a lot of his (youth) teams, but in those cases I was his coach, not his dad. Whatever he was going to do, he was going to follow the rules and do it the right way."

When that first game church-league basketball game came, Josh played the way his parents thought he might. After the game, they told him he hadn't held up his end of the bargain and he wouldn't be going back. Josh pleaded his case. He argued for another chance and promised again that he'd play hard, take it seriously and get something out of it.

Mom grudgingly obliged, but with a condition. If Josh fell in with the crowd again, he'd be without a ride home.

You might be able to guess how the second game went. Josh remembered "not playing hard, screwing around a lot and shooting the ball every time down the floor. I think I scored 40 points, but I knew I was in trouble."

And 30 or so minutes later, he was running home – mom following closely behind. It wasn't a light jog, either. The Egners live exactly 2.6 miles from First

Friends Church. Mom would pull into driveways to keep an eye on her son, let him make 50 or so yards of progress, then pull ahead into another driveway.

Josh huffed, and he puffed, and he pouted. But when he finally made it home, a lesson had been learned.

"A deal is a deal," Teresa Egner said.

****

Four years later, the deal Mike Fuline made with his players was simple.

"Just give me your best," he told them. "Whether it's in the summer, or in practice, or in a game that we're losing by 30. Just keep giving your best. Keep working. Whatever the ceiling is, let's reach it."

Fuline was named head coach at Stark County's Jackson High School in the spring of 2005, when Egner and his classmates were in seventh grade. He dived in head first, meeting with parents and players at every level and investing heavily in the youth program. He tried to lay the foundation for a successful future while putting together a varsity team that could compete in Federal League, perennially one of the toughest in Ohio.

He had a long way to go. On January 6, 2006, the defending state champion (and soon to be back-to-back champion) McKinley Bulldogs beat Fuline's first Jackson team, 99-40.

It's not as simple as saying a scant 59-point improvement was all it was going to take for the Jackson Polar Bears to reach the top of the Ohio high school basketball mountain. It was going to take years of work and commitment. It was going to take a special group of kids, a rare level of unselfishness and more than a little bit of luck — both the kind you fall into and the kind you have to chase for at least 2.6 miles.

It was going to start with a belief that it could be done.

"A crazy thought, huh?" Fuline would later say. "I knew I was going to ask for effort, for defense, for improvement. I knew we had some players coming. I knew we had good people in the community. But I didn't know where we'd end up."

A small-town kid with small-town values (he still lives in the house he grew up in), Fuline actually hesitated before taking the Jackson job. He wondered if, at 29, he was ready. He wondered how his family – and his family-oriented approach to building a program – would fit in Jackson. His in-laws were in the middle of building a house in Rootstown in Portage County, where Fuline was the head coach of a successful small-school program. Every Saturday, still, his in-laws take Fuline's four children and watch them. That was a comfortable situation that was tough to leave.

Though he was coming off a district-title season at Rootstown, Fuline wasn't sure he'd get the Jackson job. Some candidates used the opening to better their current teaching and coaching situations. When it became clear that Fuline was a strong candidate, he wasn't even sure if he wanted the job. To the outside world, high school basketball is not what it is in Stark County, where it's second only in importance to ... high school football.

Fuline called Jackson Athletic Director Terry Peterson because he was going to withdraw from contention. Fuline's grandmother had just died and his wife gave birth the day of Fuline's interview. He wasn't sure if he wanted the job, and certainly was in no state of mind to make that call.

Peterson talked him into staying in. Ultimately, Fuline ended up being offered the position. He was an up-and-coming coach taking over a program that had proven success, but had fallen on hard times.

Fuline had a tough sell on his hands. Larry Taylor, the man whom Fuline replaced, lorded over the Jackson program. He was clearly in charge at all times. It was his program that had made two state-tournament appearances.

Now Fuline was selling family values to people he didn't know. He wanted his players, and their families, to buy into the team concept. And he had to get families in an upper-middle class, white-collar community to buy in. The Jackson community would get Fuline's family — two sides of Italians with roots in Youngstown — and he, in turn, wanted theirs.

What needed fixed first, though, was Jackson's youth basketball program. Today there are close to 500 young basketball players in the Jackson Youth Basketball Association, a program that runs like a machine. A youth program is the lifeblood of any successful high school program, producing players with strong fundamental skills and big dreams. A couple of those kids cut their hair like Egner's Mohawk this winter.

A successful high school program – one with good kids, good players who are good role models, and one that wins on Friday nights – feeds the dreams of those young players. Fuline had grown up in that environment in nearby Manchester, a place that won the AAA state basketball title in 1974 and still has plenty of people who talk about it like it happened two years ago. He'd been an above-average player on successful teams there and still maintained close relationships with his friends from those teams. He maintained close relationships with players from his time as an assistant coach at Green, and he'd seen just about everyone involved with the Rootstown program quickly embrace his "family" approach there.

He had crazy dreams, dreams that included taking Jackson to places his Manchester teams or the successful teams coached by his beloved uncle, Joe Fuline, at Struthers had never been.

Believe it or not – and he often privately chose not – he had people in Jackson who believed the scores would change, the records would improve, the opportunities would come.

****

This was March 2010. This was Mike Fuline, running late because he'd squeezed a quick trip home to see his four children in between practice and a scouting trip. His Jackson team was the top seed in the always-tough Canton Division I District tournament but ranked just 13th in the final Associated Press state poll. This was a team that had made marked improvements from year to year but still entered a season of high expectations having not won anything, having not cut down a net or even playing for a district title.

The conversation in Fuline's truck started with an old friend talking about the benchmarks of success this Jackson team had a chance to pass, how potentially winning a district title over the likes of McKinley or North Canton Hoover would be one heck of an accomplishment in the now and raise the bar for the future.

Fuline was listening. He was acknowledging his friend's words. But he wasn't settling.

"You only get so many of these chances," he said as he wound his way through the back roads that mark his path from home to the Canton Civic Center. "Columbus. We want to get to Columbus."

That path to Columbus started in Columbus, of all places, in the summer of 2009. Jackson won the team championship at the Ohio State Team Camp, twice defeating defending big-school state champion Columbus Northland, a team that would be ranked atop most national prep basketball polls for the majority of the 2009-10 season.

But the Northland team Jackson defeated was without its best player and one of the best players in the country, reigning Mr. Basketball Jared Sullinger. It was a big step for the up and comers, but it was just one.

There were many more ahead, but they'd have to come one at a time. Fuline hoped his talented big men, Mark Henniger and Josh Egner, would sign their full-ride scholarship letters of intent early enough that recruiting wouldn't be an in-season distraction. They did. Henniger signed with Kent State, and Egner inked his with Akron.

He hoped his point guard, Brad DuPont, would continue to make the steady individual improvements he'd shown in the spring and summer. He hoped his other guards would come back stronger, more confident and more ready to handle the rigors of a long season and the pressure, both internal and external, than they had the season before.

He hoped playing top competition all summer, not just in that one camp, would pay off. He hoped all his players understood their path to anywhere might require them beating Hoover, their backyard rival and the team that crushed Jackson's hopes the previous season, as many as three times.

He hoped that "family" concept he'd been preaching since this group of seniors was split into two eighth-grade teams would finally take shape. That meant no backtalk or backstabbing, no individual achievements trumping team goals, no steps backwards. It was going to mean work, and trust, and higher achievement. It was going to mean role players playing their roles and the big boys playing big – much bigger than they ever had before.

He hoped the improved maturity he'd seen at various times in various settings would manifest itself on the court in the form of limited turnovers and Henniger and Egner avoiding foul trouble. He hoped that "family" thing meant he could count on Egner and DuPont controlling their tempers on the floor and on the bench, for every time one of them pounded his fist on a chair during a game, Fuline would deal with his four-year-old son, Anthony, punching a chair every time something didn't go his way at home.

More people than ever are watching, he preached. More people than ever are counting on you guys for big things, he told them. And that meant the other seniors, C.J. Julian, David Devine and Nathan Kanam, embracing their roles. That meant junior sharpshooter Michael Shull playing like a senior. That meant junior backup post players James Feller and Tyler Graening being ready when needed, without knowing if that would be once a month or once a week.

He didn't know how this season – the one that would include a trip to San Diego, a regular-season game in the arena that hosted the state tournament and ultimately a chance to win the games everyone remembers – would go.

He just knew these chances didn't come very often.

THE MVP

Sometimes people literally fall into their futures.

Such was the case with the guy who became Stark County's best player.

Despite being born three weeks early, John Mark Henniger, II was 20.5 inches long – and his father, a lifelong Los Angeles Lakers fan and fan of sports in general, had a feeling his first born would be the basketball-playing type.

But as John Mark grew into a tall, pleasant and quiet youngster – and started going by "Mark" – he didn't exactly take to basketball. Or any sport. His younger brother, Josh, seemed to love every sport and was always on the run with the other neighborhood kids when the Hennigers moved back from Texas to Stark County when Mark was in fifth grade and Josh was in fourth.

Mark played youth baseball, but he was never really into it – at least until he took a fall off of his skateboard and ended up with his strong hand, his right, in a cast.

"Mark liked video games," David Devine said. "Josh and I played everything all day long and we'd try to get Mark to come out and play baseball and basketball and football with us. And most of the time, he would just ignore us altogether."

"We had just moved back from Texas, and I pushed him pretty hard into basketball," his father recalled. "He went out and skateboarded and broke his right wrist. But I can remember it seemed like every night he'd be out there in Price Park in North Canton, shooting with his left hand.

"Did I ever think he'd stick with it and become the player he did? No. But I knew if he was given the chance and he worked at it, he might be pretty good."

John grew up in nearby Perry Township, the son of the man who'd been the pastor at the Canton Baptist Temple for 42 years. He met his wife, Deborah, when both were students at Bob Jones University in South Carolina.

The Hennigers lived in North Canton when the kids were young. John worked for his father in Canton for 17 years before getting a church of his own in Arlington, Texas. When the opportunity to become a pastor of his own church closer to home, in Barberton, the Hennigers say the quality of the school system was the most important factor in their picking Jackson.

By the time they were settled, Mark was plenty into basketball. But in the big business that youth basketball has become, John and Deborah were worried about finding a fit for their sons.

"When we moved back from Texas, we were starting anew," John said. "As far as basketball, even at an early age kids had roles and places and teams were already formed. That was concerning. Even though I could see the potential in Mark, we appreciated that the other kids accepted him. That was a big thing. "

****

While the other kids who'd eventually become the core of the history-making basketball team played other sports, Mark Henniger played only basketball. He developed slowly, but surely, physically and as a player. He always effectively could use both hands near the basket, and by the time he entered high school he was almost 6-foot-5.

"He was a guard through grade school and into middle school," Fuline said. "I know he played AAU with a lot of guys who grew up to become fine players, guys who at the time were probably much quicker and better than he was. I think that's probably when he developed a lot of the fundamentals that eventually helped him become such a good post player.

"He'd tell me all the time at practice, 'Coach, I was the best 3-point shooter on those AAU teams I played on with C.J. McCollum (the 2010 Patriot League Player of the Year) and (GlenOak High School star) Storm Sanders.' And I'd tell him, 'Mark, I hope someday you'll be a great 3-point shooter again. But that day is not today.'

"Not having seen those AAU games, I don't know for sure, but I'd bet that he adapted to whatever style he needed to. He always had this knack for kind of quietly finding a way to make a play."

Doing almost everything quietly was Mark's specialty – at least when authority figures were around. Fuline recalls a young Henniger responding to the chance to play varsity as a freshman by …

yawning in the locker room during pre-game speeches.

"I came to know he didn't mean anything by it," Fuline said. "But at the time, I didn't think either one of us was going to be long for Jackson basketball."

Calm and quiet had always been Mark's preferred approaches.

"We don't know where he got that," Deborah Henniger said. "My husband and I are both very intense, very aggressive people. I remember Mark playing baseball in second grade and the coach wondered how he never got upset. I thought that was the norm – that's just how he was all the time."

"I remember we'd play some wild middle school games in those tiny gyms, the kind of game when everybody is all fired up and yelling and at the time it seems like the most important thing in the world," his father said. "Mark would be out there tangled up with a kid who was stronger than him, he'd have coaches yelling at him, parents yelling at him and he'd go to the foul line with the game on the line.

"I'd be up there red-faced and yelling, too, and he'd turn and smile at me. That's his way of handling stress."

Mark said he never meant to offend anyone – especially not Fuline – with his laid-back demeanor. He came off the bench to average 8.5 points and four rebounds as a freshman while battling the likes of 7-footers Kosta Koufos (a former first-round pick of the Utah Jazz) and Kenny Frease (Xavier University) in the Federal League.

"Those were real eye-openers," his mother said.

Even if Jackson's young stud was wiping his eyes when his team took the floor, Jon Perdue remembers a district tournament game Henniger's sophomore year against undefeated Timken.

He said Fuline played on the David vs. Goliath theme in delivering a pre-game speech "that made you want to run through a wall. I think we all had chills. It was a moment I'll never forget and everyone was so pumped up that I knew we were going to come out firing."

The intensity and focus were evident as the players gathered and waited for the official start of pregame warm-ups. Or so Perdue thought.

"We're standing at the top of the stairs, waiting for the horn to sound to take the floor," Perdue said. "I'm fired up. The kids are all fired up. Right to the side of the doorway is this Zamboni-type machine they use at the Civic Center for some of the other events they have there. It's parked there, not even where anybody who's staring at the floor would be looking.

"And Mark looks at me and says, 'Wouldn't it be so cool if I could just drive that Zamboni right now?'

"That's Mark. That's just how he's always been."

Imagine if he'd never fallen off that skateboard. Fate stops for no one.

"To this day he'll come home after a game and I'll say, 'Good game. By my count you had 22 points and 12 rebounds,'" his father said. "And Mark will say, 'Wow, that sounds pretty solid.' He had no idea. The stats are the last thing on his mind.

"As a father, that allowed me a lot more joy than somebody out there counting them."

THINKING BIG

Jackson assistant coach Tim Debevec has plenty of ticket stubs from plenty of Ohio High School Athletic Association's State Basketball Tournaments. Until this year, he'd never been a part of one. He'd never been in the program. Never been on the floor. Never introduced before the game.

He watched still-famous teams at his alma mater, Barberton High School, make multiple trips to the state and regional tournaments. He played for the still-famous Jack Greynolds Sr. at Barberton, and coached alongside his son and close friend, Jackie Jr., for many years and at multiple stops.

He's a basketball lifer, and he's darn proud of it.

"I have the job I have because of basketball, I got my wife through my best friend because of basketball, I got my college degree and I'm working on my second Master's because Jack Sr. always told us to get an education and have another plan," Debevec said. "He'd tell us that no matter what it was, Plan A wasn't usually going to work. He'd say, 'There's no harm in learning something.' Jack got me through college because he made me work.

"He was just a motivator. He was much more a teacher of life lessons than an X-and-O guy on the court. I got kicked off twice; suspended for two games for lying to him. He didn't care if you started or scored 40 points a game, if you lied to him or didn't hold up your end of the bargain, he was going to suspend you. Some kids don't like to learn lessons, but the good ones learn them and grow."

Debevec believes there are four ingredients most teams that make the big-school state tournament share.

The first is luck, "because even teams with four or five studs need some bounces along the way. Maybe the tournament draw is kind to you. Maybe the referees are kind to you one night. Whoever you are, there are too many good teams to think you're going to crush everybody and have your A-game every night for three weeks when tournament time comes."

The second is a good summer, not just in seeing individual improvement, but in building chemistry and a winning mindset. When Jackson went 37-2 in the summer of 2009, losing only to a Mentor team they'd see again and a team of college players and incoming recruits at the University of Michigan camp, he told Fuline he was getting good vibes.

"But I wasn't getting too excited," Debevec said, "because I knew how hard it was going to be. Still, any really good team I'd ever been around started with a really good summer and carried over."

The third – and maybe the "biggest" reason he wasn't afraid to share his excitement – was his belief that the big-school tournament was a big man's game. Having two skilled players at 6-foot-7 (and growing) in Henniger and Egner would give Jackson as good a shot as anybody.

"In Division I, you're always going to run into a private school or a public school that has kids that transferred in. Every one of those teams has big guys," he said. "If you want to dream with them, you've got to have the size they have. If you've got a good point and two bigs, you've got a chance. So we knew we had a chance."

But the fourth was something many who just see the games or don't know the players intimately might not fully realize. "You've got to have guys who love the game," he said. "You can't just have big guys or a certain amount of guys who have Division I scholarships. You've got to have guys who work to get better, guys who play roles, guys who don't get caught up in any outside crap. Just play the next play, play the next game, win.

"When I played at Walsh College, we won a lot of games and had a lot of guys with unbelievable talent. But one of our best players never even picked up a ball all summer. He didn't love the game; he was just really good at it. There's a difference, and when the games get big, it shows up."

****

That he knew a thing or two about those big games was a reason Debevec was Fuline's first hire upon getting the Jackson job in the spring of 2005. He'd coached under Greynolds Jr. on Division II regional-qualifiers at Tallmadge and later followed his friend to GlenOak, one of Jackson's Federal League rivals. He also coached a year under Randy Montgomery at Hoover.

Jon Perdue had already been a young assistant at Jackson, and Fuline immediately liked his passion for the game and tireless work ethic. "He was a younger version of my dad," who would also have a seat on the bench, Fuline said.

"Jon puts the time in," Fuline said. "He's not afraid to have an opinion that maybe other guys don't originally want to hear. And he's so organized. This is a big job, and he and (freshman coach Scott) Studer both take care of so many things that make my job easier."

After the '08-'09 season, junior varsity coach Harold Fisher became the head girls basketball coach at Jackson. That opened the door for Mike Bluey, who previously coached under Fuline at Rootstown and initially came with him to Jackson, and Bluey had head-coaching experience of his own.

"I think we had a nice mix of guys with different experience, different expertise," Fuline said. "I think we all grew together and improved together. Originally only Tim and Jon knew our league. Now, we all share ideas on almost everything. Even Bluey lets me have the kids work a little bit on a two-three zone defense when he knows I'll never play it.

"With (Debevec), we had coached together at Green (under Mark Kinsley) for a year. He was a good player way back and still has great passion for the game.

He was with Randy and Jack, two great coaches in this league, and he brought experience. He was a winner. He played under Jack Sr.

"And the guy can talk to anybody."

That he can.

"When I was a player at Barberton, we ran miles in the offseason and Jack Sr. called it conditioning," Debevec said. "But it wasn't physical; it was all mental. If you couldn't handle him yelling at you in the offseason, how he could he trust you in a tight game? He ran off kids that were phenomenal players.

"Kids that played for Jack, they went to college. They didn't get fazed when little things went wrong. Come in 10, 15 years, Josh Egner will be crazy successful. He will have a good job in whatever he wants to do because he works hard. That's the lessons I've learned from basketball, if you love something and work at it, there's a payoff at the end.

****

Fuline, too, is a basketball lifer. His father said he was breaking down game film as early as sixth grade.

He admired his uncle, Joe, whose long career at Struthers High near Youngstown included a pair of district titles. He met his wife, Amy, when both were 18 and she quickly knew that sticking with Mike would mean sticking with basketball.

"I didn't even like basketball," she said. "But I liked him, so I gave it a chance. And it grew on me. Part of the reason it did is because he had so much passion for it. It's never been a job to him; it's more of what he loves and what he does.

"When we were young, he'd go from Kent State to go watch his uncle's team at Struthers. The next week we'd go to Akron and watch Manchester play. He'd say, 'Maybe this isn't what you were thinking for date night.' And I'd say, 'Hey, whatever floats your boat.'"

Amy said Mike does "as best he can" when it comes to leaving whatever frustrations basketball might bring him out of the house. But if you ever drive by the Fuline house and see the two oldest children, Gia and Anthony, tackling each other in the side yard, know the situation is under control.

"They're imitating Josh and Mark jumping up and chest-bumping each other before the games," Amy said. "They're already hooked."

****

Debevec can talk. And there's wisdom in his words.

"Those Tallmadge teams we coached, all they were missing was the height," he said. "John Maddox could shoot the lights out but he was 5-foot-8. Alan Bock was a dynamite point guard but he was 5-foot-5 on a good day when he wore tall shoes. Those guys were phenomenal players, legendary up there. But you have to have big guys."

Debevec believed in Jackson's big guys. He appreciated their skills and knew their importance. But the Jackson coaching staff encountered a problem.

They'd all been guards themselves. At least at first, no one seemed comfortable coaching Josh and Mark.

"It was a struggle," Fuline said. "I never really played with a true big guy as a player. But the biggest thing was just experience. Playing Mark as a freshman, he

33

developed and I think our staff developed in how to coach those guys."

"In the fall we'd go wherever we could and watch college teams practice," Perdue said. "I sat at Michigan State and I wrote down every single drill their big men did. Same at Duke. We figure if Coach K at Duke and Tom Izzo at Michigan State are doing it, it'll work for us.

"Obviously those guys (Henniger and Egner) kept working. Josh's work ethic is phenomenal. And Mark made so many strides. Between his sophomore and junior years, I would play at open gyms, and in the first two years I could push him around and make him do whatever I wanted. By the end, he was that much stronger. He took himself to a different level."

Fuline also believes experience is a great teacher, and he's now actually thankful that some of his Jackson teams were short – in stature and on talent – because the class of 2010, then young players, got invaluable experience.

"If we were good those years, Mark and Josh never would have played as much as they did," he said. "Brad the skinny sophomore and Michael Shull as a tiny freshman? That was the key, they played. We came to this year and it was like, well, there's no excuses. This is your time."

And both Henniger and Egner seized the opportunity.

"Every single night Mark got 20 points, 10 rebounds, he blocked shots. He was the biggest change for us," Fuline said. "Maybe other people have a different opinion, but I think his game went to a different level as a senior. He was fully consistent.

"That fire was burning. Quietly, quietly, quietly … it was burning in him. I had not seen that out of him. Whether that was satisfaction of him signing (at Kent), knowing the chemistry was good, whatever it was, it was like the perfect storm inside of him.

"He was so good that as a coach you kind of put him aside. Even when he's having an off night, he's pretty darn good. That's a great feeling."

Egner's storms were anything but quiet. He, too, took his game to another level and seemed to save his best for the biggest moments.

"Josh knows the game," Fuline said. "He's always played against great players (in AAU) and challenged himself. With his mix of ability and basketball IQ, I could coach him differently. Mark, very rarely did I yell at him because first of all he didn't like that approach. I'd call him and we go have a heart-to-heart and watch tape.

"There were times I'd make Josh really mad on purpose because I knew he played better when he was like that."

Debevec said Egner "could be a knucklehead, but man would he compete. We had to let him be him. You can't control every detail. Mike letting these guys be themselves, that's a big reason we won a state title."

Perdue said Egner was the "smartest basketball player on the team, by far. He knew matchups, he knew defenses, he knew schemes. Most of the time he was two steps ahead of every other guy out there."

Said Fuline: "You can't teach what Josh has. He'll mature physically and emotionally, but I don't want him to lose that swagger. He just thinks he's better than everybody and most of the time he's right."

THE DOMINANT DEFENDERS

Charles James Julian was born on November 26, 1991, a 7-pound, 6-ounce ball of energy. The only member of the 2010 state champs whose parents are Jackson alums, C.J. was actually born with a Massillon football in his crib. In Massillon, every male child born in the city is given a tiny Tiger football because football takes a backseat to nothing there.

Julian had a vision to score touchdowns for the Tigers, not baskets for the Polar Bears.

His father, Troy had been a swimmer "and never went to a Jackson basketball game." But he'd been in raised in a family of die-hard Massillon football fans to the point that he and his wife, Diane, had wedding pictures taken on the field at Paul Brown Tiger Stadium. On the mantle in their home is a picture of C.J., his younger sister and all their cousins dressed in Massillon football jerseys.

"All these years I spent just wanting Massillon to win a state championship in football," C.J. said, "and here I end up winning one in basketball. Pretty good deal."

When Jackson played Massillon in the sectional basketball tournament, the official start to its state tourney run, C.J. tipped a ball in Massillon's basket during a scramble at a point when Jackson had the game in hand.

"I'm pretty sure his grandmother paid him to do that," Brad DuPont said. "But even if she didn't, I think he still wanted to."

Stark County is the greatest.

The Julians' oldest child nearly lost his fingers when he got them jammed in a La Z Boy before his third birthday, and he kept his parents on the run constantly. By middle school, he'd been invited to play basketball and baseball with the guys who'd eventually become his high school teammates, and he made an immediate impression if for no other reason than he never stopped.

"C.J. was spastic," Dean Devine, David's father, recalled. "Very fast, pretty good at everything he did, and just was the Energizer Bunny."

Troy Julian said he thought his son would go on to be a high school swimmer. "He was a pretty good one." But when the time came to make a choice, he chose basketball.

"I knew it wasn't going to be baseball," Troy said. "I remember one time the kids were young, and Josh (Egner) was pitching to C.J. and he plunked him pretty good. Josh's father came and apologized to me up and down. I said, 'Gary, really, it's fine. My kid hits two or three people every single game.'"

C.J. said he really started believing in his basketball future when he and his teammates won the Federal League Freshman Tournament in 2007. With Henniger and Egner playing up, C.J. actually played some center.

"He was all arms and legs, but he competed and rebounded like crazy," the coach of that team, Scott Studer, said. "A lot of what you saw in the state championship run, you saw then. He would defend. He would hustle. He wasn't the most skilled player but he was fearless."

That limitless energy was going to have come out some way, some time, so often using it while guarding the opponent's best player turned out to be a positive for C.J. and his teammates.

"I'm not afraid of anybody," Egner said. "But I think the one kid in the state of Ohio who I wouldn't want to guard me would be C.J. Julian. He's just a real pain in the butt."

The highest of compliments from the highest of leapers. But they weren't the only ones.

"C.J. might have been the biggest goofball on the team, but don't mistake that for him not being smart," assistant coach Mike Bluey said. "He knew what was going on in the flow of the game. He knew when he had the green light to shoot and when we really needed him to get on the floor and make a play. He was all effort, all guts, all the time. "

"As a coach, my favorite stories are the ones of the young guys, the little guys in the youth program, all of a sudden started liking defense because they liked C.J. Julian," Fuline said. "He averaged what, five points a game? But he was so valuable because he just never got tired, never let up."

When Julian did need a breather – or when an elbow sent for him a quick sew-job, as it did in the regional semifinals – Fuline had another reliable glue-guy waiting on the bench. That was David Devine.

****

The less-heralded of Jackson's "quiet guys" envisioned it.

"It," of course, was winning the state championship. And it wasn't just something David Devine worked on for a couple hours after school each day. It was something for which he'd made years worth of sacrifices. Which made it OK to daydream during those long school days.

"It's a pretty good thing to think about," he said. "But doing it, that was even better. I just remember a bunch of screaming. We actually won the state championship. I don't even know what we were screaming, but it was so loud you couldn't even hear. So you just screamed louder."

In his daydreams, Devine saw his team upsetting heavily-favored Columbus Northland. He saw himself making a jumpshot, grabbing a key rebound, dishing off to Henniger for a basket plus a foul. In reality, he was asked to do all those things at various times for this team. He did them well.

Devine, who's now off to Ashland University's outstanding baseball program as a pitcher, always was playing a sport of some sort. His parents, Michigan natives who came to Stark County when the Timken Company recruited his father in the early 1980's, remember their oldest child as a toddler holding a basketball or wearing a catcher's mask. He had a Fisher-Price basketball hoop, and as he grew up he was willing to try just about any sport.

His career as a quarterback included a broken hand, a broken finger ... and not many victories. He played on traveling baseball teams with Egner and DuPont, and as their high school careers progressed he's the only one of the core basketball group to stick with baseball.

In the summer, that meant long days and tough choices. It meant perfecting the art of changing clothes in a moving car. There were times he'd have two games of each in a weekend, maybe a baseball game in Painesville, and an hour later a basketball game in Canton.

"My offseason goal was definitely to start," said David, who would ultimately become the sixth man. "But Coach always told me it's not who starts, it's who finishes. If accepting my role was part of what it was going to take for us to go to Columbus, I didn't care if that role was only to have water ready for Mark and Josh."

"I think he learned that the hours, they pay off in some way," his mother, Kelly, said. "If you really love something and you really work at it, you push the obstacles to the background. And in the end they shared this with the whole community. Kids they grew up with playing basketball were all painted up and rooting for them. They all worked for it; they all earned it."

David earned his way by listening to every little detail of the coaching he received and giving his best physical effort every time he stepped on the floor.

"David Devine has this gift for always being in the right place at the right time," Bluey said. "It's not luck, and it's not all athletic ability. It's just a mindset, an all-out effort and the sign of a kid who's smart, who listens and knows that one little play, one steal or rebound, can win you a championship.

"I don't care if he never got in the box score. He made a play every single game that helped us win."

Perdue, who often led the way in breaking down opposing personnel, called Devine "smart as heck. If I told him on Tuesday a kid on the other team was left-handed and loved to shoot from the deep right corner, he'd remember that on Friday and try to beat him to that spot."

And he played a big role in that swarming defense.

"In a lot of other years he could have been a starter," his father Dean said. "But he performed the way he needed to and held no bitterness. He gave 100 percent. He stayed ready even if he didn't know when exactly he was going to be called upon. I'm pretty proud of that.

"He got head-butted three times. That told me he was playing the role of pest pretty well."

NICE KID, DEADLY SHOT

Of all the things Mike Fuline did in his first few months on the job at Jackson, becoming the unofficial president of the unofficial Michael Shull Fan Club would turn out to be one of the most important.

"Great kid, always smiling, nicest kid in camp and one of the hardest workers," is how Fuline recalls Shull, who would have been entering seventh grade at the time. "Those things are a very good start. And he had this textbook left-handed stroke on his jump shot. I knew he was going to be my guy."

He soon found that Shull was an absolute gym rat; that textbook jump shot was no accident. It was a product of hours and hours of work in his driveway with his father, work that had been happening on an almost nightly basis since Michael was in middle school.

As Fuline's first summer as Jackson coach approached, he passed along a 25,000-shot summer workout he'd been given by his friend Mark Schlabach, the head coach at Berlin Hiland High School. The plan called for a player to shoot, over the course of the summer, 25,000 jump shots from various spots. When a parent's signature verified the work had been done, the coach would award the player with a prize of some sorts.

Shull shot 40,000 jumpers that summer. And he probably would have shot that many without the paperwork or a prize being involved.

"I grew up in Indiana loving basketball," Doug Shull said. "I was never a good player myself, but I loved it. But even I never loved it the way Michael always has. I was always watching, and he always had a ball of some sorts in his hands. I didn't push it on him. He just fell in love."

"I remember Michael being barely old enough to walk and he'd plop himself in front of the television next to his dad, who was watching college basketball," Janie Shull said. "It's hard to say if he really knew what he was watching, but he was mesmerized.

"Whatever basketball gifts he has, I think he was born with them."

By middle school Michael was not just playing all the time but winning all the time. In fifth and sixth grade he was playing on local travel teams and AAU teams that always seemed to play for championships, if not win them. He gave up baseball — "the pace of the game was too slow for me," he said — and committed himself fully to chasing his basketball goals.

With the 40,000 summer jump shots out of the way, Michael sat down and made himself a list of goals before his eighth grade basketball season began. He taped them on the wall over his bed so they'd be the first thing he'd see each morning and the last thing he'd see before flipping the light switch each night.

He had individual goals, goals for his team, goals that included classroom success matching the success he'd have on the court and enough personal growth and improvement to be ready to play varsity ball the same year he entered high school.

"That's pretty serious," Fuline said. "A kid who takes things that seriously and pushes himself like that is a coach's dream."

Shull got varsity minutes — and tasted a little success — as a skinny freshman. He wasn't fast or strong enough to be a big-time scorer, but he made some jump shots and gained valuable experience. He was the first man off the bench as a sophomore, but he struggled to find consistent success. He was a good enough shooter to make opponents' scouting reports and draw defensive attention, and the other parts of his game needed polish. He was part of the group of Jackson guards that watched Hoover's Nyles Evans — Shull's longtime friend and AAU teammate — dribble circles around and through the Polar Bears in that district semifinal loss.

And so he wiped the slate clean in the spring of 2009. He shot more jump shots than ever in the driveway and rededicated himself in the weight room. He stared at the goal sheet and talked to Fuline about the disappointment he felt.

"When I went to talk to Coach (in the spring of '09), he already knew we needed to have that talk," Shull said. "I knew I had to improve tremendously, but I knew I could do it. He believed in me, and I believed in myself."

"There was no question to me that Michael was capable of better," Fuline said. "And knowing the way he worked, I knew he would get better. He didn't shoot it as well as he's capable of at the end of his sophomore year, but I don't think he lost confidence. I just think he needed to know the older guys believed in him."

Shull wasn't just one of the guys; with Egner and Henniger drawing so much attention underneath, he was one of the open guys on the perimeter. He started knocking down wide open 3-pointers in the summer and making the Polar Bears even tougher to defend.

And in October, just weeks before the quest for the state championship would officially begin, he taped this new list of goals to the wall.

- Play like I know how to play
- Be a silent leader
- Make our team have better overall chemistry
- Get better at individual skills
- Work hard every day
- Become stronger and quicker
- Do my strength routine every day
- Win the Federal League
- Make it to states
- Keep a 3.6 or higher GPA
- Be the guy everyone respects and looks up to
- Keep all goals in sight. Do them all everyday.

Every day, he read them. Every day, he worked at them.

A stronger, more confident Shull had a knack for knocking down first-quarter shots that not only softened up defenses but got Jackson's wild student section going. He became a defensive pest, took care of the ball with more authority and more confidence and had the green light to let it fly when it was open.

"I was really the only junior who played a lot, but I was one of the guys," Shull said. "The only time Josh yelled at me was when I didn't shoot the ball."

With one state title in the books, it will be interesting to see how his goal sheet changes as he prepares for his senior season. But there's little doubt he'll put in 40,000 shots worth of work, continue to improve and continue to get the most out of himself. It's not just about getting to March for Michael Shull, who already even has a distinct vision for his future — college, then chiropractic school, then his own chiropractic practice.

"Unless I grow eight inches," he said. "If that happens, I'm going to play in the NBA."

HALFTIME OF FURY TURNS SEASON

Everyone has a breaking point. Mike Fuline reached his on January 16, 2010. Half of the season was already in the books and the Polar Bears were cruising along to a 10-1 record. Hardly the tipping point it would seem.

But Fuline knew his team was capable of so much more. Jackson had the makings — two talented big men inside, a solid point guard in Brad Dupont, a shooting guard who could live up to the title in Michael Shull and a defensive specialist in C.J. Julian, along with a host of role players — of a team that could pose matchup problems for just about any team they'd see, in Stark County and well beyond.

But the Polar Bears, despite all the talent and expectations, didn't have a tangible shred of proof they were any good. They had a belief and hope, but those are things that can be touched and felt. They were still the team that hadn't won a darn thing yet.

After watching them play like a team that wasn't going to win a darn thing in the future, either, in the first half on January 16, Fuline had enough.

The Polar Bears hosted Timken in the biggest game of the night in Stark County. The Trojans were athletic and talented. They could match Jackson's athleticism, but not Egner and Henniger's height. The Trojans had beaten Jackson the last two years in non-league games and were good enough to beat many teams badly.

"They had our number the last couple of years and it was January and we played some really good teams up to that point," Fuline said. "We went out and played timid in the first half. We're a good team on our home floor in front of a sold-out crowd and we didn't play with any fire."

The Jackson High gym was packed to capacity, 2,200 people crammed in to watch what was supposed to be Jackson's best effort of the season. Instead they watched 16 minutes of a game — the one that kicked off the second half of the season and a push to a state title — in which their team was intimidated. Scared. Not of TImken, but perhaps of success.

"I really don't think they knew how good they were," Fuline said. "People who saw us later in the year in Columbus, saw us at our best. That's the best we played. That's how we practiced. That's how we played a lot of good games against teams in the summer. We were just treading water during the season just to get to March. After the Timken game, we finally got a little swagger. It was something we could refer back to. It was something we could touch. It was more than hope now."

On a night the Bears were supposed to own, they looked like an unmade bed in the first half. They were out of sync. They had little passion.

This was their gym. Their crowd. Their moment. Their season. And yet they went into the halftime locker room down by six, 31-25, and probably should have been down by more.

It was a halftime that would change their season, and help shape them into young men.

****

Fuline is an easy-going coach. He's the kind of guy players love to play for. He can still relate to his players. He isn't fire and brimstone. He is more big brother than fatherly figure at 34 years old and a locker room full of players about half his age.

His players relate well to him. Even-tempered and soft-spoken, he's always quick with a joke to diffuse a tense moment. There is a story that has followed Fuline since he was a kid. It proves how he never takes himself, or a situation, too seriously.

He was a kid, a young teenager when he decided to move his parents' car out of the garage and in the process he wiped out the driver's side of the car against the garage. Dan Fuline, his father, was seething. Mike looked at him, smiled and said, "Someday you're going to laugh about this." And there Dan Fuline was at a dinner telling the story after Jackson won the state title and everyone in the room was laughing.

This, however, wasn't one of those times to laugh. What was supposed to be Jackson's season of dreams was at a crossroads.

Losing to Timken didn't matter in the Federal League race. But this game was about two weeks before the sectional-district tournament draw. A loss to the Trojans would mean Jackson quite possibly could be the second seed, instead of the first. Aside from that, the ramifications were more about growing up.

****

As soon as the locker room door slammed shut, the atmosphere was different than any kind Jackson's team had been in before.

Fuline started in on his players. The words came out of his mouth faster than his brain could process them. Before long, he had screamed so loud and so long that his voice was gone. His mouth was moving. Only air was coming out.

"I was about to start hyperventilating," Fuline said. "I don't scream a whole lot. I just lost it. I was frustrated. I don't think they realized how good they were. We played with no energy. We played scared. I told them that wasn't good enough. It was time to see if we were ready to become men.

"This was our moment. It was right there. There are moments in a season, moments in a life when you decide which way things are gonna go."

Fuline picked up one of the wooden stools that are in front of each players locker. He threw it down. Perhaps it would smash into pieces and emphasize his point. The stool didn't shatter. Fuline hurt his thumb.

Still, no one laughed. As easy going and carefree as Jackson played the season, this wasn't the time.

This was, in fact, their moment. This was a lesson to be learned along the way.

"I don't remember the exact words, but it was something I'll never forget," said DuPont, who scored 14 points in the Timken game. "He was yelling, but it wasn't just anger. He threw the stool down. We all got the message that he was really ticked off. This was our court. This was our chance to send a message to every team in the district. He got to us.

"You could tell it was coming from his heart. He was challenging us. We were either as good as we wanted people to think, or we weren't."

That's a tough challenge to live with. Jackson was either a facade or it wasn't. The Bears were either the best team in Stark County or they weren't. It was their decision in the middle of January in the middle of the season.

Fuline might as well have been a traffic cop at a fork in the road. There it is fellas, you decide.

"We were all jacked up about it and we went out and just pounded them," DuPont said. "That was the turning point of the year."

Sometime between that stool bouncing (but not breaking) on the carpet and dominant second-half run that produced a runaway win, a beast was awakened from a slumber.

"We were tough individually, but this was the first time all season we were tough collectively," Fuline said. "You could see toughness in Brad, Josh and Mark at times. This was the first time everyone was dialed in and refused to let us lose.

"Now that they'd seen what it was like, no one wanted to let it go. We were waiting as a coach staff to put it all together against a good team. We wanted to see if we could do it. We waited for two and a half months. This was the first time we showed how good we were on in a game with a lot people there to see us. We played like we were capable."

In hindsight, it was a blessing that the Polar Bears waited two and a half months to play that way. No one wants to take the court like their playing for a state title in November. Maintaining that pace is a recipe for failure. Jackson peaked at the right moment: halftime of Timken game.

Early in the third quarter, Egner caught a long pass from DuPont, sidestepped a defender on the baseline and jammed the ball through the rim with two hands. The crowd got into the game and cut Timken's lead to 32-29. On the next offensive possession, Jackson broke through half-hearted defensive pressure by Timken and Henniger took a pass near the key, dribbled through the lane and threw down a rare dunk.

The gym rocked. The Jackson faifthul went crazy when Henniger completed a three-point play with a layup and free throw on the next possession. Egner pounded his chest and looked at the Jackson bench. Henniger was business-like. The entire team was.

Their mission was starting.

You could practically feel the Polar Bears becoming men, or at least the team that would lead a community to a state title. A six-point deficit turned into a five-point lead. Then 10. Then it was out of control. The Bears went on to beat Timken 75-53. It was their finest half of the season, including the state championship.

By dismantling Timken, they proved they could be as good as they thought they were.

"We told them there were a lot of people out there on our side and it was time to go out in the second half and become men," Fuline said. "We won some big games prior to that. But this was a mental hurdle we had to get over. We played two games in San Diego against really good teams. We'd beaten North Canton before. We beat McKinley at McKinley. We were undefeated in the league, and this was a team we hadn't beaten in two years."

When the basketball season ended in March with Jackson holding the Division I state championship, that wasn't the same team that played in January. The Bears played some of their best basketball in the summer before the varsity season started. But they never played with the confidence and swagger they finished the season with until they beat Timken.

All year, though, Fuline wanted something tangible his players could see. He needed to show them proof they were good enough to win it all. Jackson went to

San Diego and blew a big lead against Mentor to lose in the title game of a tournament. The team was dejected in the locker room. The coaching staff hurt so badly, after the game they walked from their hotel (Mentor was staying there and it was celebrating the win), still dressed in their suits and through a steady rain to find dinner.

"We went to San Diego trying to win something," Fuline said. "We hadn't won anything tangible. Against Timken, that was our moment to set out to accomplish something. At that point we stopped hoping and started making things happen."

Every player in the rotation played an integral part that night against Timken. Shull hit a couple of reverse layups. Julian and David Devine played in-your-face defense.

When it was over, the locker room feeling was quite different than it was at halftime. There wasn't a sense of relief; rather a sense of accomplishment. Fuline never tipped his hand to the media of what happened at halftime.

"We're getting there," Fuline told The Repository. "It's getting better. It's starting to look like the team we saw in the summer. It's this simple with us: When we play together and trust each other, we're pretty fun to watch."

The Timken win and the Mentor loss 2,000 miles away are linked. In California, a big lead slipped away. That was a devastating loss.

"Being in that locker room, it looked like someone kicked us in a really bad way," Fuline said. "But I made sure we all knew something. We got on our knees and I had them look at me. We went to California and we didn't get our goal. But we get to fly on a plane and go home and still accomplish our goals to win our league and get to Columbus."

FATHERS AND SONS

Before Brad DuPont left a lasting imprint on the Jackson Basketball program, he left a forever-lasting imprint in the drywall of his family's basement.

His older brother had a hand in both.

Jay DuPont was a Jackson basketball player himself, a starter when Brad was a freshman and a guy who was usually replaced a few minutes into the games by the skinny and sleepy-eyed Mark Henniger.

Fuline remembers Jay the 6-foot-2 basketball player as "a big guy who wasn't very big, but he played hard. He fought."

He fought with his brother, too. When Brad was just eight or nine, a game of one-on-one basement basketball turned into a game of football, which just happened to be Jay's sport of choice. This particular tackle turned into both a catapult and one his family would talk about for years.

"I remember being upstairs and hearing this crash," John DuPont said. "I didn't want my wife to freak out, but I was pretty sure I knew what it was.

"I remember going downstairs to see what exactly was going on. When I got downstairs there it was – a perfect outline of where Brad hit after flying through the air."

Some lessons are learned the hard way.

"A lot of our games ended up in wrestling matches," Brad said. "And when I got my butt kicked, I probably did deserve it."

Whether he realized it or not, Brad DuPont learned toughness – and probably a bit of humility – by being the younger, smaller brother. He became a relentless leader and rugged competitor among kids his own age, and he was always driven by the goal of first running with and someday surpassing his older brother in a variety of capacities, especially on the athletic field.

****

Fuline knows the feeling. He, too, was the younger of two boys who grew up playing basketball, football, baseball, golf – just about everything. He's two-and-a-half years younger than Dan Jr., who played center on Manchester's first-ever state playoff football team in 1989.

"I always remember that because that's the first time I ever thought of my brother as a friend," Dan Jr. recalled. "The first playoff game was at Jackson, which is a weird coincidence, but he was the first person to jump on me after the game and give me a hug. I'll never forget that.

"He was a freshman then. A lot of kids that age are too cool for their own good, but he was genuinely happy for me."

Dan Fuline Sr. said he never thought his sons were too competitive, except for the "standard brother vs. brother confrontations, mostly messing around." They both played on the highly-successful Manchester A's traveling baseball team; Dan eventually became a very good football player and Mike later started on Manchester's basketball and baseball teams – teams that more than hold their own when stacked up against others in the small school's rich athletic history.

"We weren't cutthroat competitive all the time," Mike said. "But deep down, there's nobody I wanted to beat more than my brother.

"That changed when we got older and he kind of became my biggest fan. He'd drive home from Kent State for my high school basketball games and he'd be there in the front row coaching me up. He'd leave notes around the house encouraging me and telling me to visualize success. I might even be guilty of taking a little advantage of the fact that in his eyes, the little brother can do no wrong. He's always had my back, always will."

It was family first in the Fuline household, but sports were a close second. Dan Sr. coached Mike's CYO basketball team – he remembers details of the sixth-grade championship season like it happened last week – and has been a fixture on the bench for teams Mike has coached the last dozen seasons since he was at Green High School.

Two years ago, "Papa," as he's known around the Jackson program, tore his meniscus during a game "trying to will a shot in the bucket." Neither son was the least bit surprised.

"My dad has a lot of energy," Dan Jr. said. "I'll never forget being in high school, waking up all tired and kind of sleepwalking out of my room. He would be sitting there drinking his coffee and all of a sudden he'd jump up and get in a three-point stance. I wasn't even in the shower yet but he was telling me to get my game face on."

Said Mike: "I think he did that when it wasn't a game day, too. The guy just loves sports and loves life."

Of the adults closest to the program Papa Fuline was probably the biggest believer — at least outwardly — that the 2009-10 team would reach its highest goals.

"And I tried to tell everybody else it was going to happen," he said. "This group was so tough, so resilient. Sometimes they drove me crazy because I felt like they waited until they had to before they turned it on, but they found ways to win."

And to make believers out of everybody.

"I am a realist but I also love the fact that the unthinkable can happen," Dan Jr. said. "I knew what was at stake. My hope was that they would win the league, hopefully the district and then see what would happen in the regionals. I guess I just wanted them to be healthy and not have anything happen, just so everybody involved would get a fair shot.

"When we played (Huber Heights Wayne) in Columbus, Northland played the very next game and I watched them. I thought if we got back to Columbus and played them that we would get crushed. Everybody but my dad thought that. He argued with me for the next two weeks.

"I knew this Jackson team was special. I knew it would be a memorable season. But if I ever thought they'd win the state championship, I would have bought a video camera last summer. I might have bought a few of them."

****

Big Brother DuPont kept the faith. And he stayed on Brad.

Jay made the trip back from Pittsburgh, where he's finishing his bachelor's degree, for all of the state tournament games, and the wonders of modern technology helped him stay close to his brother even when he couldn't physically be there.

"It was great that this whole thing brought us closer, but he did act like my dad a little bit," Brad said. "He would text message me all the time: 'Get to sleep, make sure you're eating right, you guys can do this.'

"It's really cool that he was able to make it home as much as he did. I know there were some nights he'd drive back to Pittsburgh at 2 or 3 in the morning because he'd have a test at 8 a.m., but he still came to the games. I can actually talk to him now, but I have to remind him he's still just my brother. He kind of likes to be dad."

Both DuPont brothers are glad to have their dad share this time, too. Brad was in the midst of his eighth-grade basketball season when John DuPont was diagnosed with advanced prostate cancer, a diagnosis that said he might have just six months to live.

Everything changed, from day-to-day life to long-term priorities. Brad said he turned the anger from the uncertainty of the situation into positive energy on the basketball floor but admitted it was a lot for a teenager to take on. Speaking at the post-state championship reception, Sue DuPont said she spent many sleepless nights wondering if her husband would be able to see her son and his teammates chase their state-title goals.

John DuPont's cancer is now in remission. He said his favorite memories of Jackson's magical March aren't necessarily of swinging his shirt over his head, but of sharing those postgame hugs with Brad.

"After the St. John's game he told me that one was for me," John said. "It's a moment I'll never forget."

"Right now it's a story with a happy ending. It's something that's extremely awesome for our family and for him," Brad said. "Everybody's ecstatic. We're all proud of him. He still has checkups at the Cleveland Clinic and he's still getting good news."

AVOIDING DISASTER

A strange thing happened on the way to Jackson-Hoover, Part III for the district championship.

Lake started kicking Jackson's butts.

Lake, a team that had won six in a row but was still just above .500 for the season. Lake, a team that had been run out of its own gym by a Jackson team just starting to find its stride in February. Lake, a team that could not match Jackson's size in the paint or quickness on the perimeter, decided it would play smart, aggressive, carefree basketball from the jump of this district semifinal.

Jackson was content to watch. And miss. And play a step behind. The Polar Bears opened the postseason by blowing out Massillon and showed up to this one thinking it would be more of the same. That thinking was wrong.

"A nightmare," Shull said.

"The worst half of the season," said Brad DuPont, who joined Henniger in being saddled with two early fouls and was just one of many guys in white jerseys to throw up bricks during a 1-of-12 second quarter.

It was almost fitting that C.J. Julian's parents, who were in Washington D.C. as part of the National Honor Flight program for which they'd often volunteered, started losing their Internet connection and the broadcast of the game. Like many Jackson fans who were actually in the Civic Center, they started to panic.

"C.J. told us to go on the trip," Diane Julian said. "And here we were, eight hours away, thinking we were going to miss our son's last game. I was telling myself I was a terrible mother."

"I was telling myself that all the people who thought Jackson always choked were going to be right again," C.J. said.

A terrible first half ended with a 30-18 Lake lead. A very sparse crowd in the Jackson student section lamented its potential fate. The locker room, at first, was silent.

"I never doubted that we could win that game," Henniger would later say. "But we didn't leave ourselves any margin for error. We had to turn it on right away."

Fuline, too, believed his team could come back and win. He stressed defense, and guts, and urgency in his eight-minute halftime speech. He told his players they'd come too far and worked too hard for it to end here; he stressed that he believed in them, but as he made the long, dazed walk up the stairs and back to the bench, he wondered what he would see.

The lesson he wanted his team to learn: Every team has a bad half. Tough teams fight through it and advance.

The lesson he hoped it wouldn't learn: March, the greatest basketball month of the year, goes by fast. It goes by even faster if you get eliminated on March 10.

****

Killing the unlikeliest scenario – tenth seeded Lake actually eliminating the top-seeded Polar Bears – really came via a shot by the unlikeliest of heroes.

The third quarter started with a pair of 3-pointers from Shull that cut the deficit to six. Then Henniger got going, but it was Jackson's swarming defense that really sparked the change in momentum and a muscle-flexing 17-0 run.

"I don't think they got the ball past the foul line in the first seven minutes of the third quarter," Shull said.

"I'm pretty sure that's no exaggeration," Fuline said later.

Lake's only points in that third quarter came on a 3-pointer with 15 seconds left, making it 35-33, Jackson. DuPont came quickly the other way and found nothing open under the basket against a Lake defense that certainly wasn't going to give Jackson an easy one. But with time running down, he threw a pass along the baseline to Nathan Kanam, who was spotted up in the left corner.

Swish.

It was the biggest shot of the season for Kanam, the steady senior guard who played the fewest minutes of the players in the rotation.

"That was just me doing my job," Kanam said of the shot. "I had to stay ready for that situation. I set my feet, and it felt good when it left my hand. It turned out to be a big shot for us."

The shot pushed the Jackson crowd into a frenzy for the minute break between the third and fourth quarters. Kanam's older brother, Jonathan, was listening via internet radio feed in Columbus and sent his father, Duke, a text message that said, in a nod to popular Cleveland Cavaliers broadcaster Austin Carr, "Kanam hits from deeeeep in the Civic Center."

"Just a great moment for Nathan and for the team," Duke Kanam said.

And another important lesson: Pouting about individual playing time or accomplishments gets the pouter a whole lot of nowhere. Staying ready just might pay off.

"As much as I wished I would have played more and I certainly think I did well when I was called upon. I understood my role," Nathan Kanam said. "Coach made it very clear to us that the way we were going to succeed was to have everybody accept his role. Mine was to push Brad and Michael in practice and to stay on top of things for when my chance came.

"I knew I could contribute. At the time I wasn't over thinking it, but I knew I could make that kind of big shot."

While his teammates had had pretty much given up playing other sports, Kanam played football and ended up being a two-time state qualifier in tennis. He found time to maintain an overall 4.6 GPA, good enough to rank him third in Jackson's graduating class of almost 500. He also scored a 30 on his ACT.

"Probably higher than the whole coaching staff combined," Debevec joked.

"They don't make 18 year old kids sharper or more impressive than Nathan Kanam," Fuline said.

At a school like Jackson – where the competition and standards in the classroom are as high if not higher than they are on the athletic fields – Kanam's accomplishments are especially impressive. He said he pondered giving up one of his sports at times and actually did give up baseball after growing up playing on top-level travel teams with Brad DuPont. But in the end he decided high school was too short for him to give up just being a kid.

"I might play football or tennis in college," he said. "But it won't be anything like being on a basketball team with my friends from elementary school and the whole community being behind us. Maybe we don't realize now how special this whole experience was, but we will."

Kanam was the brains of the operation, but he also fit into the fun-first atmosphere in which the players thrived. He would often break the monotony of long practice weeks with impersonations of the coaching staff – comedic work that was so good, word of it spread quickly.

"He was the man of impersonations," Fuline said. "I never saw his Coach Fuline impersonation, but I heard about it. And the ones I did see had me laughing for an hour. When he had a cheeseburger in his hand and was impersonating Coach Perdue, I almost fell out of my chair."

Before the '08-'09 season, Coach Perdue snuck into Kanam's hotel room while the team was out of town for a camp. When Kanam got out of the shower, his roommates prodded him into doing his Perdue impersonation.

"I kind of hid behind one of the beds," Perdue said. "And I laughed so hard that I couldn't hide anymore. I sat up and Nathan got red as red can be. He was embarrassed, but it was spot-on. And very funny.

"I have all the respect in the world for that kid. He's a successful, competitive person. It's not easy for an 18 year old kid to play a background role. But the whole year he accepted that and stayed ready. It's a tribute to his character."

****

Jackson would take control of the Lake game, maintaining a lead of between four and seven points throughout most of the fourth. But in a wild sequence in the final 40 seconds, DuPont absorbed a hard foul near halfcourt and ended up chasing the offender 40-some feet, all the way behind the Jackson basket, to confront him.

DuPont got hit with a technical and was lucky his teammates and officials got there to separate him before he picked up another, which would have brought an ejection and a suspension for the next game. The technical foul shots cut the Jackson lead to two.

"I lost my cool," DuPont said. "I know I almost cost us the season."

The Polar Bears survived, though, and emerged as a family. Not a happy family, but one that would live to play another day thanks to its defense. And shots from Shull and Kanam. Egner seemed to grab every board, and Henniger scored 12 of his 22 points in the fourth quarter.

Even the Julians had a better second half. They abandoned the spotty internet connection and had friends at home in North Canton who propped the phone next to the radio so they could hear the comeback. And the technical. And, ultimately, the joy of a victory that lacked style points but ended with Jackson having seven more points than the hungry underdog.

"We came out flat; we underestimated them," C.J. Julian would later say. "Maybe we didn't deserve it for the way we played, but we earned it. And we came out of there thinking that if that didn't beat us, it was going to be tough to beat us, period."

Twenty-four hours later, Hoover turned in a workman-like effort and pulled away from McKinley to set up the district title game everyone had been expecting. The morning of the game, Jackson's hot-headed point guard woke up to find a note from his warm-hearted mother.

They're coming for you Boo…like "white on rice."

They plan to frustrate the hell out of you.

They're going to try and 'decapitate' the head …

Get you in foul trouble or better yet, kicked out of the game.

But they are in for a BIG surprise - they will <u>not</u> be successful … Not tonight.

Tonight I know you will be in control of the situation. You will laugh at their attempts. You will use their game plan as further motivation to get lots of assists.

You will remain calm and super confident. You'll remember that great players get this kind of 'attention'…players like Michael Jordan and LeBron.

And like them…you will lead your team and find a way to achieve your goal! <u>Believe</u> …and you will achieve. Enjoy the journey!

FINISHING THE HOOVER SWEEP

Hoover's gameplan wasn't going to be much different than it was in the first two meetings. The Vikings wanted Jackson – especially DuPont and Egner – to have to play a slower, halfcourt game. They would pressure DuPont, bump him, prod him and try to close his passing lanes. If they got him to lose his cool in the process, that was a bonus.

That's what Mom was worried about.

Jackson's gameplan wasn't going to be much different, either. Throw it inside. Run at every opportunity. The Polar Bears maybe didn't have anybody as quick as Hoover point guard Nyles Evans, but they had an overall quickness edge. And they had more shooters. And better bigs. A steady, poised effort would bring a chance to officially bury last year's demons and win the district championship.

The district title would be Jackson's first since 2001, when the Polar Bears also went on to win the regional tournament and qualify for state. This group of seniors was in third grade then, and Brad Dupont calls going to watch Jackson play in Columbus one of his greatest childhood memories.

"I can still name all those guys," he said. "It was just an awesome experience to look up to them, to have them coach us at camps, then to go see the lights and the scoreboard and 15,000 people watching them play at Ohio State. It's something I decided right then I was going to do."

"We came home from Columbus," John DuPont said, "and every night Brad would be out in that driveway until 11 o'clock, just shooting, playing, having his own state tournament."

A young Brad saw his own state tournament as one in which he'd be the brightest star. Jackson's all-time assist leader now isn't afraid to admit that he was once was allergic to passing.

"When I was younger, a lot of parents used to tell my parents I was too cocky and I was a ball hog," he said. "I developed into a passer. My parents would tell me after games sometimes that I was being a ball hog."

Eventually, Brad listened.

"He was always very good, very determined," Sue DuPont said. "But he was also always making sure he got his points. I remember having a talk with him and saying, 'I watched Larry Bird, one of the greatest players ever, and he took as much pride in making a good pass as he did making a big shot.' I don't know if he was listening at the time, but eventually it stuck."

His parents weren't the only ones who noticed Brad's talent at a young age. He was so good in Jackson's youth league and at the high school program's summer camps that some of the coaches actually started to slant the playing field.

"If we didn't do something," Jon Perdue said, "he would win every drill, every time."

This was fifth and sixth grade, when most kids were still learning the fundamentals of the game. When travel teams were being built, Brad DuPont was the prized free agent. But when the high school coaches were involved, they wanted every kid to feel he had a chance to succeed.

"We didn't cheat him," Perdue said. "But we knew if we gave him good teammates, he was going to win. Brad plus one other good player and that was a lock, give that team the trophy. If there was a ball-handling competition, he'd win. If there was a shooting contest, he'd win. We were always weary of him winning everything and leaving the other kids discouraged.

"He was a little more advanced skill wise and he was physically more developed than most kids. But it was that competitiveness, even back then, that really separated him. It's that fire he still has today."

That fire that almost cost Jackson the Lake game earned Brad a special talking-to from his head coach, but that wasn't the only time such a conversation happened. Fuline always had a special place in his heart for point guards, not just because he was one himself but because "a point guard is your coach on the floor. That's cliché, but it's true. I needed to be able to depend on him in every situation."

Perdue said he often referred to Brad as "Mini-Me" because Brad reminded him of himself as a player. "He was more skilled than I was, but we had the same mindset," Perdue said. "Hard-nosed, always on the floor, not taking any crap. He was a bulldog for us."

DuPont wore number 20 not necessarily because he wanted to, but because it's the number Fuline and

Perdue chose for him. It's the number both of them wore during their high school careers. It's also the number of wins Jackson had entering the district final.

****

Getting to 21 – and getting the biggest one – wasn't going to be nearly as easy as Jackson made it look in the Federal League Championship Game. But the Polar Bears came out aggressive and confident, dominated the glass and created transition opportunities. DuPont's coast-to-coast layup beat the halftime buzzer and gave Jackson a 31-19 lead.

But Hoover had shooters. And tournament veterans. And once Evans started getting into the lane, a 10-point fourth-quarter lead was quickly cut to six. And then four. The momentum swung. The orange-clad side of the packed Civic Center crowd went nuts. Linda Fuline, Mike's mother, went into hiding.

She left her seat in the first few rows and retreated to the hallway, unable to watch. She was trusting her ears, but she didn't like what she was hearing, either. As the tempo slowed and it turned into Hoover's kind of possession-by-possession game, Mike Fuline implored his team to trust its defense to provide a spark and turn the tide. With 1:40 left, Hoover cut the lead to 53-52.

But the Vikings wouldn't score again. Josh Egner's blocked shots made sure of it.

****

Egner wasn't always a leaper. In fact, he was a very average athlete when he was younger.

"I was fat," Josh said. "No need to deny it now. I was fat, and even when I started to grow out of it I was too slow.

"He was never a great athlete when he was younger," Gary Egner said. "He was a smart kid, and he always worked. But it was hard for him because his athletic ability hadn't caught up to his growing body. I thought at some point he'd grow into his huge feet, and he might have a chance to be good then."

****

Here were Josh and Teresa Egner again, again with the car pulled over to the side of the road.

This was almost seven years before this district title game and almost four years after Josh ran home from a church-league basketball game, mom following closely behind, when Josh didn't hold up his end of a deal they'd made about giving his best. This was Josh, no longer a pudgy youngster but a tall, skinny freshman with a season of high school junior-varsity basketball under his belt and a chance to play for the prestigious King James AAU team – yes, LeBron James' team – in the spring.

He had given up baseball and put the frustrations of a miserable eighth-grade year of basketball behind. He'd been disgruntled enough that he'd both considered quitting basketball and transferring (to Hoover, of all places), but instead he'd decided that he loved basketball too much and was part of a group with too much potential to do anything but fully throw himself into it.

So here he was, asking his mom to pull over, hopping out of the car and throwing up in a ditch on Wales Road after another workout at High Intensity Training in Green.

"That's when I knew he was really dedicated," Teresa Egner said. "Not that it makes for a good story because I pulled over and he'd throw up, but that he wasn't scared of the pain or the sacrifice. He really wanted to play for King James and play varsity the next year, and I think he had to convince himself that he was ready. He was going to work.

"He'd have to change his shirt on those rides home too. He didn't have any puke on them, but even 30 minutes after the workout he'd still be sweating so much that he'd soak right through the shirt."

It wasn't just the first time. Josh would leave his lunch somewhere near the same spot after several subsequent workouts. But his transformation from average athlete to one of the most memorable dunkers local high school hoop fans had ever seen was underway.

"I was so slow and unathletic, it had to be painful to watch," Josh said. "My body was changing so much and I didn't know if I'd ever keep up. In seventh grade I was fat – Coach Stu still has the pictures and makes fun of me – and then I got taller, kind of just grew out of being fat and I really loved basketball. But I wasn't anywhere near strong or quick enough to play the way I wanted to play."

"I liked to keep him a little humble and keep that program picture handy," Scott Studer said. "He was chunky. I remember coaching him the summer after his eighth grade year. He could block shots but he wouldn't jump out of the gym. He still had a lot of work to do with his post moves and shooting.

"In the next few years he was always jumping up and grabbing the rim. He jumped all the time, and I think the other kids kind of made fun of him for it. But once he started dunking in games, he got the last laugh."

He got the last laugh in the district final, too, first as he and Henniger each blocked a shot in the same possession in the final 30 seconds. Then Michael Shull got fouled with Jackson up, 53-52, with 10 seconds left.

The kid who shot more of these shots in his driveway each summer got a talkin-to from his fiery point guard on his way to the line. "I won't repeat what Brad said," Michael said. "But I knew I had to make them."

He did, making it a 3-point game. Hoover's Cory Veldhuizen had his game-tying shot blocked by Egner in the final seconds and time expired. The Jackson team stormed the floor. Linda Fuline returned to her seat. For the first time since these players were wide-eyed elementary school fans, Jackson was going to the Sweet 16.

BRINGING IT HOME

A wild celebration was breaking out all around Mike Fuline. The Jackson coach was celebrating a Division I regional championship win over Toledo St. John's. He was celebrating with players, their parents, his parents, his family. He was celebrating with anyone else who wanted to.

The Polar Bears had just punched their ticket to the Division I state tournament.

But they would be long-shots, at best, once they got there. Columbus Northland had, supposedly, the best team in Ohio, and it had the best player in the state. The media, and Internet-indulged fans some times get a little carried away with labeling high school basketball players.

Besides, rarely does it ever work out the way most people think it should. Who had Jackson winning it all before the season started?

"They're kids. You talk about it," Fuline said. "You always talk about getting to Columbus. We talked about it."

Talking is one thing. Believing is another.

"We truly beat a good basketball team in Toledo St. John's," Fuline said. "But even then, it felt like we'd been there, we'd done that. We'd beaten good teams during the season. I still knew we weren't playing our best basketball.

"By the time the tournament started, it was just nice to play a new team. The night we played Massillon, Mark Henniger said it. He said, 'It's so nice to play someone new.' We were excited to play a new team. In the Federal League, everyone knows each other so well. They know your strengths and tendencies. But you get to the regional tournament, and everyone's new."

Still, who really thought on March 20th, Fuline, Henniger, Josh Egner, Brad DuPont, C.J. Julian, Michael Shull and the rest of the Polar Bears would be in the middle of the University of Akron's JAR Arena court jumping up and down celebrating a trip to Columbus?

Maybe a couple of fathers and diehard fans. Coaches and players don't really think in terms of winning a state championship. It is a goal, like making it across the finish line at a marathon is a goal. Both are so far down the road, however, all the competitor really thinks about is the next mile.

But on this March night the next mile was here. The finish line was in sight and the next best runner had just tripped and fallen.

Fuline stopped celebrating.

Someone had pulled him aside and whispered something in his ear.

Columbus Northland, the team with Jared Sullinger — one of the best players in the country — had just been upset. While Jackson was celebrating the improbable, Northland — two hours away — was dealing with a crushing defeat. The two teams were mirror opposites of one another. At the right time in the right season, Jackson's players were growing together tighter and they were believing more and more in their coach's family theme. Northland had come apart and its season came crashing down when Gahanna Lincoln laid a 71-45 spanking at the Ohio Expo Center.

"It just wasn't in the cards (that night)," Satch Sullinger told the Columbus Dispatch immediately after the game. "This wasn't the team I coached all year but a lot has to do with Gahanna. I just don't know. All it takes is one hiccup. We lost to a quality team that just shot the lights out. That's nothing to be ashamed about."

About 120 miles north, Egner was telling reporters after Jackson's win, "This is it for us. This is our time. This was supposed to happen."

But Egner had the same feeling everyone else associated with Jackson's program did. When Northland lost, the door swung open for Jackson to win it all. Everyone would think the Polar Bears were an underdog and Fuline nor any of his players would try to argue otherwise in the week leading up to the game. If people wanted to believe that Gahanna Lincoln and Cincinnati Moeller were that much better, let them.

After the regional championship win, Egner hugged his mother, Teresa, on the court. He told her, "Northland lost tonight. We're going to be state champs."

Teresa Egner wasn't ready to take anything for granted. She'd just watched Jackson survive two close games in the regional. She told her son they could be sharing the same kind of hug, only bigger, exactly a week from now if things worked out.

"He said, 'Mom, there's no could be. We are going to be,'" Teresa Egner said.

In that moment when word traveled north of Northland's demise, the state tournament took on a new meaning for Jackson. Not only was the Polar Bears goal touchable, it was realistic. In all fairness, a Northland matchup would have been created a tough obstacle because Northland might have been able to defend Jackson's inside presence of Henniger and Egner. Northland had two Ohio State commits on the block, a Penn State-committed point guard and a backup post player who, as a sophomore, has a scholarship offer from West Virginia.

But Northland wasn't a factor.

Fuline stopped in his tracks as soon as the whisper registered in his head.

"It was a whole new perspective at that point," Fuline said. "We'd just one the regional final and we're on the floor celebrating. As soon as I found out Northland lost, it went from elation to 'Let's go.' I don't know what that was, but it was a slap in the face that, 'Hey man, this is the chance. Things are falling into place.'

"I think we'd have given Northland all they wanted. Now it was like, 'Holy crap, we're going to win this thing.' If Northland would have been in it, we knew we'd be major underdogs, but we were going to play our butts off. Now we went into the state tournament with four teams evenly matched."

Evenly matched?

By the time Monday afternoon rolled around, Fuline still had a tired look on his face. He and his coaching staff enjoyed the fruits of their labors Saturday night. Sunday morning, Fuline and Athletic Director Terry Peterson headed to Columbus for a state tournament meeting and to get Jackson's portion of pre-sale tickets. Fuline spent the rest of the day trying to track down Gahanna Lincoln film.

He had a working knowledge of the team Jackson would play Friday night. The Polar Bears knew Lincoln's point guard Stevie Taylor was the team's engine. He made them go and how Taylor went, so did Lincoln. Egner played with Taylor in a summer AAU tournament. Inside the locker room, the scouting report that made its way around was Taylor did not like to be physical and he did not like in-your-face defense. Funny thing is DuPont could specialize in that.

But Taylor was not the only concern. In the Northland win, Lincoln shot better than 60 percent. If Jackson allowed that to happen, the Bears would head to Columbus one-and-done.

There was plenty of reason to be concerned about Jackson's chances in Columbus. The Polar Bears almost lost in the regional semifinals to Akron East, a team many believed Jackson would handle. But the Bears struggled all night and the more they struggled, the more confidence East had. Before long, Jackson's season rode on a last-second East layup that didn't go in. Jackson won that game 58-56 and the tough loss drew one of the season's more memorable quotes from an opposing coach.

"We're not very big. We don't shoot exceptionally well, and we're not very well coached," East head coach Ross Fiorello said. "But our kids bust their (butts), and they play with a lot of heart, and they overachieve."

East struggled at the foul line that night. It hit just 50 percent from the charity line. Perhaps without even knowing it, Fiorello ignited Jackson players.

"It takes a combination of talent and toughness," Fiorello said of winning in the tournament. "I thought how we played was enough to get it done. That's a hard sell to these kids. They don't see mental toughness at home. They don't know what the hell I'm talking about when I say it."

That was a compliment to the way Jackson kids are raised.

These are the lessons learned on the way to a state championship. Some lessons start at home.

When the game was on the line, and their season, the Bears played tougher when it mattered most. Henniger had a go-ahead layup late in the game. What most people missed was Julian setting a screen that opened the play up for Henniger. Julian also took an accidental elbow to the head from Egner in the second quarter. The elbow opened Julian's head. He took stitches at halftime to close the wound and then got back out on the floor.

"Talent isn't enough," Fuline said. "Don't think we felt like, 'We're Jackson and let's roll the balls out and go play.'"

The next game was against Toledo St. John's and it was for a trip to Columbus. Egner started to hit his tournament stride in Akron, where he will play his future college games. Henniger was steady. Jackson got past St. John's by a bucket, too, but the outcome of that game never seemed to be in jeopardy, at least not as much. A memorable DuPont-to-Egner alley oop all but sealed it.

Once the Bears punched their ticket to Columbus, no one knew it at the time, but the heavy lifting was finished. Jackson would never be in another street fight on the basketball court like it was in the district and regional tournaments. There were games — Lake, East, St. John's, and maybe even Hoover — that could've gone the other way. In Columbus the Polar Bears laid it on the opposition and won a state title by a combined 35 points.

"The district tournament was tougher than the state tournament," Fuline said. "It was tougher in a lot of ways. Obviously, we wanted to win our league. When we did, there it was, out first trophy. That was our first trophy together."

Fuline, huddled with players and parents the night Jackson clinched the league trophy, cried. It was the only time he cried after "winning something."

"I didn't get emotional after we won it in Columbus," Fuline said. "After we won the Federal League, we stayed after. We presented each other T-shirts. People say you got more emotional for winning the league? Absolutely in this league.

"The district tournament is a mental hurdle as much as anything. You know if you get through the district, you have a chance in Columbus. Whoever gets out of the Canton district, has a 100 percent chance to get to Columbus. That was one of the things that appealed to me about this job. If you want to get to Columbus, you know the teams you have to beat. It's right there."

That's why Columbus seemed like a breeze. Jackson players had prepared all season for tougher games. In a week, all they had to do was beat two teams they didn't know much about, and the teams didn't know much about them.

One of the first things the team talked about during practice the week of the state tournament was Gahanna's record. The Lions were 26-0. They were undefeated for a reason. Jackson respected that record. It respected Gahanna. After beating Northland they way Gahanna did, it was fair to wond all week if the same was true on the other side.

Before the game, Fuline laid it all out for his players in a posh locker room at Value City Arena. "Everything has been a puzzle," Fuline said in a locker room that was quiet and all eyes trained on him just before tip-off. "Your whole high school careers have been a piece to the puzzle to get to this point.

"It's here! Look at me! It's here! "The hard part is over! Now you go have fun. Let yourself loose!"

And late in the third quarter, DuPont had a break-away steal. He could have easily converted a layup. Instead, he went for style points and created a play that will be remembered in state tournament lore. DuPont lobbed the ball off the backboard and Egner came flying through the lane and jammed it home. The thunder dunk made the arena erupt. Heck, even Gahanna Lincoln fans were cheering.

"People say it takes stones to try a play like that," DuPont said. "It felt normal to me; felt like it had to happen. I've thrown that pass to him before. I don't know if it was a harder play. It's one that we'll remember, though."

The funny thing was, that was a play that Egner and DuPont practiced in a shoot-around the morning of the state semifinal game.

"This isn't scary," Fuline said in the locker room. "The scary part was playing Lake in the district. This ... you earned this. Now go take what's yours. If you play like you did against St. John's last week, you win it."

The hardest parts were well behind them. The players were exhausted once they returned to the team hotel. They had pizza. Some relaxed in a hot tub. Most others iced down and ate pizza.

When the players went to bed, the coaches went to work. They obtained as many copies of Moeller – which had beaten Mentor in overtime in the other semifinal -- tape as they could. Fuline had an arrangement with the Mentor coaching staff. If Mentor lost, it would give Jackson all its scouting information on Moeller. Jackson would return the favor for Gahanna. Fuline knew he wouldn't have to give up Gahanna's scouting report. Truth be told, though, the players and coaches were leaning toward a rematch with Mentor.

Out in San Diego, which was a trip that was as much about bonding as basketball, Mentor ruined things. Jackson blew a big lead in the championship game. Two Ohio teams playing for a tournament title all the way across the country, and the Bears blew a lead. Fuline still didn't have something tangible for his players to touch.

Now they had Moeller. No one seemed concerned. The coaching staff stayed up until 2 in the morning looking at Moeller. Assistant coach Jon Perdue, the resident expert on detailing opposing personnel, wrote a report for each player. Fuline and assistants Tim Debevec, Mike Bluey and Scott Studer broke down the films, traded them off and then hashed out assignments.

Jackson High School, a team from Stark County few thought would be here, commandeered the hotel lobby, two flat panel TVs and most of the tables and chairs. They were on a mission. Everything fell into place and no one wanted to regret leaving a stone unturned.

Hanging from a ceiling rafter was a hand painted sign that read, "We Believe." One of the corners fell down. Fuline motioned to a table of coaches' wives, "someone tape that back up before it all falls ... that's karma."

The next day seemed to drag on. Everyone tried to find something to do. The Bears didn't play until 8:30 Saturday night. Fuline and the coaches caught up on sleep. The players mostly stayed in their rooms after the morning shoot-around. A funny thing happened. Jackson's team vans arrived at the same time Moeller's team bus did. The players funneled down the walkway where the teams enter the arena. They squeezed through the same door. Jackson players did not look intimidated. They seemed relaxed.

This was their moment. If there is one thing Jackson learned all summer and regular season was this: When that moment arrives, grab it. If you don't it escapes forever. The Polar Bears spent all season chasing their moment.

They owned the night in Columbus. Jackson completely dominated Moeller and won 57-34. There was a point early in the third quarter in which Jackson simply broke its opponent's spirits. Too much quickness on the perimeter. Too many blocked shots. The game was over right then.

All along, they believed.

"Surreal isn't the right word," Egner said. "We kept it realistic the whole time. We knew if we caught a couple breaks this is the place we'd be in."

They'd been working for this – one of them in particular running since the sixth grade – and they'd eventually turned the Value City Arena floor into a sea of purple.

They cut down both nets. They believed.

BEHIND THE SCENES

For an entire week Mike Fuline and his administrative team at Jackson High School agreed to give inside access to The Repository for all the team's practices, all its meals and team functions. Todd Porter rode in one of the team vans to Columbus with most of the coaching staff. He ate where they ate. He slept in the same hotel they slept in.

Here is a look behind the scenes at that week, courtesy of his blog published that week on www.cantonrep.com.

Kids at Jackson High School have it pretty nice. Everything at the school is pristine. It's practically spit-shined everyday. It sparkles that way, at least. It's pristine. It's perfect.

Things are done the same way in Mike Fuline's basketball program.

Practice starts precisely at 3 o'clock in the afternoon each day during the week of the state tournament. No one is late. No one is exactly too serious when practice starts.

There is a mellow calmness about the Polar Bears. Fuline doesn't sweat the small stuff. It has worked all season long. He isn't about to fix what isn't broke days before the biggest games of his and his players' careers.

Something jumps out.

The practice shorts the players wear to each practice are black. They don't have "Jackson" or "Polar Bears" written on them.

"Family."

That's the word in block letters screen printed on the left leg of every players' shorts.

For 75 minutes the Bears are learning nuances of what they can expect in the semifinal game. Fuline tells his starting five — Mark Henniger, Josh Egner, Michael Shull, C.J. Julian and Brad DuPont — who they'll be guarding. Fuline described the opposing players with praise.

"Psychotic-great athlete. ... He's a beast. ... A great shooter. ... Every guy shoots the 3 and shoots it well. We have to contest. ... If we can't keep Stevie (Taylor) in front of us, we're screwed."

He sets the tone for practice by telling the players the coaches are going to be jerks on this last practice. They're pushed hard.

"Bust your butts for an hour and five minutes," Fuline said. "They're 26-0 for a reason."

There is a fine line in coaching. There is a fine line in playing. Believing is one thing. Expecting it to happen is another. Gahanna Lincoln was not a bad basketball team. They didn't beat Columbus Northland, and essentially open up the tournament for everyone, on a fluke. They played with passion and a purpose. It was something that caught Fuline's eye early in watching film.

Fuline is big on visualization. A scout team player drills the first 3-pointer.

"That's why we have to defend every 3-pointer," Fuline barks. "Get a hand up!"

The point is driven home. The Bears put together the best 60 minutes of practice they have all week.

Fuline praises them.

"If we play defense like that, we're playing on Saturday," Fuline said.

That is when the Division I state championship game is played. Jackson planned on being in the state title game the entire week. No one loaded on a team van and headed to Columbus to be a spectator when the Division I state championship game tipped off Saturday night. Fuline didn't even order tickets for his team to watch the game. He figured they'd be playing in it.

Every day in practice the players are reminded of what they are. Together they head to a tournament as underdogs to try to win two games few people outside Stark County believe they can.

"This summer we drove to Cleveland once or twice a week to play some of the best teams you can play," Fuline said at a community rally held two days before Jackson's first state tournament game. "One tournament was on the night of the Jackson festival. We left at 7 at night and all the players' friends, their families were at the festival. And we're on vans heading to Cleveland to play in a 95-degree gym.

"We know ... Saturday is our last game."

The crowd roared.

MARCH 29th

Forget the X's and O's. When a high school basketball team advances out of a district tournament as tough as Canton's, X's and O's take care of themselves.

Yes, the Jackson High School boys basketball team had five "prototype" starters as Moeller head coach Carl Kremer said. The Polar Bears were a tough match-up for most any team. They had two big men in Mark Henniger and Josh Egner and both moved extremely well and were athletic for their size. Both played defense without taking plays off. Yes, Jackson had a strong, quick and heady point guard in Brad DuPont. It had a shooter in Michael Shull and a defensive specialist in C.J. Julian.

What the Polar Bears also had was calm. They had a sense of comfort with one another that most teams never achieve.

Jackson ate lunch both Friday and Saturday of the state tournament at the Winking Lizard in Columbus. There were a couple small piles of snow in the grass out in the parking lot. DuPont and Egner grabbed a couple of snowballs and hid behind a parked car. Head Coach Mike Fuline, distracted in conversation with assistant coaches, walked through the front door to an ambush.

The players missed both days. On Saturday, after Jackson had 23 turnovers in a semifinal win against Gahanna Lincoln, Fuline got off a zinger at DuPont.

"I see why we turned the ball over 23 times. You can't hit me with a snowball. You throw snowballs like you threw passes last night."

DuPont laughed.

But it occurred to me: Was there a head coach in Stark County would had the type of relationship with his players. I thought through a couple of head coaches in the county. Who would have laughed, and ran to the protection of a waiting van to avoid being hit by a snowball?

More importantly, which team's players would have felt that kind of comfort level with a coach to even attempt to hit him with a snowball?

Just Jackson.

That's a big reason why the Polar Bears are state champs today.

MARCH 26th

State of mind changes quickly at the state tournament. After hitting the hotel's breakfast buffet the Jackson Polar Bears headed off to Otterbein College for a shoot-around this morning. The hour-long practice was light, but the mood was serious.

To this point, this has been a team full of teen-agers who have been together for more than four years. They've been playing basketball most of the last 12 months together. It hit the coaching staff that they're only nine weeks away from starting the next summer program.

No one wants this season to end quite yet. Jackson players were focused and quietly intense this morning. They had lunch at the Winking Lizard in Columbus. It is owned by the same man who owns the Winking Lizard in Jackson Township. He donated lunch.

Players were advised — and they listened — not to over eat. The team will be provided Subway before tonight's 8:30 state semifinal against Gahanna Lincoln.

In one of the lighter moments today, the players and coaches debated who was the better rapper. The players went with Notorious B.I.G. The coaches said no way. Tupac.

"My college roommate didn't go to class for two weeks when Tupac died," head coach Mike Fuline said.

Back and forth the argument went. Senior Mark Henniger quieted the debate by saying it was a generational thing.

Assistant coach Tim Debevec, who speaks what the rest of the staff playfully calls Barberton, rolled his eyes at one point. Debevec tends to speak quickly and one words bleeds into the next.

"Seriouslythisiswhatthey'retalkingaboutwhocares?"

The staff feels good about the team's mindset. Jackson has to play defense tonight.

MARCH 26th

Thursday's welcome to Columbus and the Ohio High School Athletic Association boys basketball state tournament was interesting … to say the least. Jackson head coach Mike Fuline was welcomed to his first state tournament by, a tow truck.

The players attended the Division II semifinal between Benedictine and Dunbar. They got an eye-opening lesson in the state tournament. Benedictine lost a 15-point lead and eventually the game.

After that, the team ate — and did they eat — at Eddie George's restaurant.

There has been somewhat of a running debate among the coaching staff about whether taking vans or a charter bus was the way to go. The team chose vans so the school provided four rental vans. The thinking was it is easier to maneuver around in vans than one large bus, and a bit cheaper, too.

At least it was.

The van Fuline was riding, but not driving, was towed. The van was parked in a lot near the restaurant. About 1,200 feet away from where the van was parked was a "tow-away zone" sign. This, unfortunately, was the van I was riding in, too.

After finding out this wasn't a joke and standing outside in the pouring, freezing rain, we finally tracked the whereabouts of the van to an impound lot owned by Shamrock towing. … Fitting, Shamrock. This wasn't our lucky day.

After making sure all the players were secured back at the hotel and leaving ample coaches with them, Debevec returned to the restaurant to give six of us a ride to the impound lot.

Now we're all fairly younger fellas. We don't carry cash. Debit card? We had plenty.

The impound fee was, get this, $140.

I had 40 bucks. Trainer Rick Neitzelt had 100. We had the impound fee.

Our plight was not over.

I have no idea what the fella's name was behind the bulletproof glass at the impound lot. Let's call him Bubba. You get the picture.

Bubba wasn't gonna let us have our rental van. At this point, it's getting close to 10 p.m. The newspaper guy has a deadline. His computer bag was impounded, too.

The computer bag was swiped when we retrieved the rental car agreement.

But Bubba insisted on releasing the car to only the person who signed for the rental car. Jackson Athletic Director Terry Peterson signed for it. Peterson was awakened, drove from his hotel near the airport about 30 minutes away, to the impound lot and alas the car was released.

Now I've written in some pretty hairy situations in 19 years. I can safely say this was the most interesting.

Today story was banged out with me sitting on a cold cement floor, with leaky cement walls in the "lobby" of the impound lot.

****

Conveniently the impound lot had an ATM machine in its lobby, which resembled a holding cell for U.S. citizens found trespassing in Iran. The fee to take out money was $5. They also had an option to get $140 out, another convenience of an impound lot.

•••••

Fuline handled the entire ordeal with amazing calmness given the fact he has to be feeling some pressure down here. At one point, after Bubba refused to give up a van decorated in Jackson's purple and gold colors with Jackson Polar Bears written all over to coaches wearing Jackson gear, Fuline asked him, "You do believe that's our car and we're not trying to steal an impounded rental car from you."

Bubba relented. He believed.

He was just following policy.

·····

Teen-age boys can eat.

And the Jackson basketball team is a smart bunch.

The OHSAA allows $15 per player/per day for meals. The plays all managed to eat at Eddie George's and then split huge deserts.

Josh Egner put away a one-pound piece of carrot cake. This thing looked like a cinder block. Most of the players hammered a chocolate chip cookie ice cream sandwich that game with like a half gallon of ice cream.

MARCH 25th

Mike Fuline didn't score a single point for the Jackson Polar Bears this season. But he is the head coach. His impact on the program is indisputable. Fuline has the Bears in the state tournament.

Jackson sold more than 3,000 tickets, which raked in well over $25,000 for the OHSAA coffers.

You'd think they'd find the head coach a closer parking spot for the Division II game Fuline and the team attended Thursday evening. Instead, Fuline's van had to park a 10-minute walk from Value City Arena, in the wind, in the rain and in the cold.

The head coach never complained. He didn't get rattled when two players were a few minutes late meeting up in the hotel lobby. Laid back.

"It's the only way to be," Fuline said.

The Polar Bears watched Dayton Dunbar and Cleveland Benedictine play in the Division II semifinal Thursday evening. After that, they went to Eddie George's restaurant in Columbus.

It isn't all fun.

Fuline has another hour carved out for the players and coaches to go over the Gahanna Lincoln scouting report. Lights are out and coaches will do a bed check at 11 tonight.

MARCH 24th

If anyone needed more proof of just how good Gahanna Lincoln is, watch the final seconds of its game against Cleveland Heights. That was a game in which Heights was winning and Lincoln came back and won.

As the closing seconds of the game are ticking away, Lincoln guard Stevie Taylor stole the ball just past halfcourt, dribbled in and converted the layup. The interesting part wasn't the layup. It was watching Rob Brandenburg, trailing Taylor on the play, double backflips and cartwheels down the side of the court as the final seconds ticked off

"How many high school basketball players can do that?" Fuline asked.

The thought occurred: How many would even try?

****

Gahanna Lincoln brought in former Ohio State and NBA player Lawrence Funderburke to help prepare the team for its regional championship game against Northland, which was the previous No. 1 team in the country.

Jackson brought in a couple of area recent college graduates to give the team a better look. Among them was former Polar Bear big man Josh Yanke.

MARCH 24th

All the intense practices are in the books. The Jackson High School boys basketball team polished off their last real practice for Friday's Division I state semifinal game against Gahanna Lincoln by putting in the last of their game plan.

Then they were treated to dinner. Quaker Steak & Lube invited the players to the restaurant for a team feed. Things turned ugly before the dinner was over.

On a dare, or perhaps plain testosterone, the team's youngest assistant coach, Brock Williams, ordered and ate a half dozen Triple Atomic wings, things that ought to come with a fire extinguisher. Williams threw down the wings, but before he was done, he was sweating and had tears coming out of his eyes.

The coaching staff wanted to know how much Williams won in the bet.

Nothing. He did it for the Atomic wings T-shirt.

Williams, who graduated from Jackson in 2003 said he was doing fine. He said his belly was gurgling a bit.

Oh boy.

March 23rd

Coaches are no different than players. In some cases, maybe a little worse.

The Jackson High School boys basketball coaching staff is a close-knit bunch. At this point in the season, practice takes care of itself. So the coaches are gathered in Mike Fuline's office, a large flat panel TV screen hangs on a wall with an NCAA basketball game on.

The coaches begin to talk about whether or not assistant coach Scott Studer can wear a suit for games at the state tournament. He hasn't been, but this is the state tournament.

Bygz, Mike Bessler the equipment manager, weighs in. Studer will wear what's got Jackson this far.

"In 25 years of doing this, I've learned you can't keep wearing the same thing to every game," Studer said.

But Bygz is superstitious.

In the corner opposite the Vizio flat panel is a pitiful artificial Christmas tree decorated in Jackson purple with cut-out Polar Bears. Bygz is afraid to take it down. The Bears are winning with it up.

•••••

How's this for student spirit? More than 2,500 final four T-shirts were sold within four hours at Jackson schools Tuesday. The initial batch of 480 student tickets sold out in an hour. The school has already sold more than 600 student tickets, which are now being sold in the upper bowl near the floor seats for the students.

March 22nd

There was a half-sheet cake in the locker room. Senior guard Brad DuPont, like a typical teen-ager, scooped of a healthy piece of chocolate cake and devoured it in his hand.

That cake has a story, though.

It traveled farther than did the Polar Bears in playing two games at the University of Akron's James A. Rhodes Arena last week, which ended with a regional championship win over Toledo St. John's on Saturday. But the cake hasn't come as far as Jackson.

Last Thursday the Polar Bears had a team meal at Carrabba's. The cake was supposed to be desert after that meal. Problem was head coach Mike Fuline forgot about it. Everything — from the meal to the desert — falls on the head coach's shoulders.

"The waitress came running out to the parking lot with it as me and my wife were getting in the car," Fuline said.

They took the cake to their southern Summit County home. Problem.

"We didn't have any room in the refrigerator for it," Fuline said.

Fuline's mother-in-law picked the cake up Friday and took it to her home in Rootstown to store it.

The cake was brought to Saturday night's game in Akron. If Jackson won, they would bring out the cake for the players and families at Gameday Grille.

"We forgot to eat it then, too," Fuline said. "That cake has been on a journey by itself."

•••••

Jackson players had Sunday off. It was anything but an off day for Fuline, his coaching staff and Athletic Director Terry Peterson. They were driving to Columbus at 7 Sunday morning for a state tournament meeting. While Peterson and Fuline attended the OHSAA meeting, assistant coaches traveled around Columbus trying to pick up scouting information on Gahanna Lincoln.

"Actually, most of us I think just relaxed Sunday," guard Michael Shull said. "That was a rough game Saturday. I think we needed a day to just sort of sit back."

Fuline is running on adrenaline. He had a tough game Saturday night. A long day Sunday. A long day Monday.

And he and his wife, Amy, have four children (the oldest of whom is 6). Giavona is 6, Anthony, 5, Lucia is 2 and Angelina is 1.

"Yeah, there's a few vowels in those names," said Fuline, who, like his wife, is Italian.

APPENDIX

Jackson's 2009-2010 Schedule and Results
Head Coach: Mike Fuline, Fifth Season, 87-42
2008-2009 Records: 17-5, 8-2
at Firestone, Won 68-46
Carrollton, Won 93-52
GlenOak, Won 76-60
at Perry, Won 64-58
at Mount Si, Washington in San Diego, Won 70-66, OT
at Chartiers Valley, Pa. in San Diego, Won 70-58
at Mentor, Ohio in San Diego, Lost 70-67a
at McKinley, Won 54-42
at Wadsworth, Won 65-51
Boardman, Won 70-44
Timken, Won 75-53
North Canton Hoover, Won 59-56, OT
at Huber Heights Wayne in Columbus, Lost 62-53
at Lake, Won 74-46
Fitch, Won 98-58
Fitch in Federal League Tournament, Won 98-39
GlenOak in Federal League Tournament, Won 89-67
Northwest, Won 100-33
Hoover in Federal League Tournament final, Won
63-44
at Green, Won 59-39
Tournament
Massillon in Sectional, Won 71-48
Lake in District, Won 56-49
Hoover in District Championship, Won 55-52
Akron East in Regional, Won 48-46
**Tol. St. John's in Regional Championship, Won
52-50**
Gahanna Lincoln in State Semifinal, Won 62-50
Cin. Moeller in State Championship, Won 57-34

Federal League Basketball Standings

	League		Overall	
	W	L	W	L
Jackson	**10**	**0**	**25**	**2**
McKinley	8	2	18	5
Hoover	7	3	19	5
Lake	5	5	14	9
GlenOak	4	6	10	11
Perry	4	6	11	11
Boardman	2	8	7	14
Fitch	0	10	1	20

Michael Shull buries a game-clinching free throw in the final seconds of the district title win against North Canton Hoover.

The Division I district champions clown around at Memorial Civic Center after beating North Canton Hoover. Pictured are C.J. Julian, Brad DuPont, Nathan Kanam, Josh Egner, Mark Henniger and Dan Devine.

Mark Henniger (40), Michael Shull (middle) and Brad DuPont play defense in a state semifinal win against Ghanna Lincoln.

Josh Egner waits for the point guard Brad DuPont to break through Ghanna Lincoln's pressure in the Division I state semifinal game.

John DuPont celebrates the only way he knows how — without a shirt. A shirtless DuPont became symbollic with big wins during the season

1st row, L-R, C. Corbett, T. Graening, N. Kanam, B. DuPont, C.J. Julian,
M. Fuline, S. Griffin, D. Devine, M. Shull, S. Rowlands, B.Johns
2nd row, L-R, D. Fuline, B. Williams, S. Studer, J. Henniger, J. Egner,
M. Henniger, W. Eisenberg, J. Feller, T. Debevec, J. Perdue, M.Bessler